SOU
KOREA

By Simon Pierce
and Laura L. Sullivan

EXPLORING
WORLD
CULTURES

Cavendish
Square

Published in 2024 by Cavendish Square Publishing, LLC
2544 Clinton Street, Buffalo, NY 14224

Library of Congress Cataloging-in-Publication Data

Names: Sullivan, Laura L., 1974- author. | Pierce, Simon, author.
Title: South Korea / by Simon Pierce and Laura L. Sullivan.
Description: [Second edition]. | Buffalo, NY : Cavendish Square Publishing,
    [2024] | Series: Exploring world cultures | Includes index.
Identifiers: LCCN 2023035038 | ISBN 9781502670052 (library binding) | ISBN
    9781502670045 (paperback) | ISBN 9781502670069 (ebook)
Subjects: LCSH: Korea (South)--Juvenile literature.
Classification: LCC DS902 .S84 2024 | DDC 951.95--dc23/eng/20230804
LC record available at https://lccn.loc.gov/2023035038

Writers: Laura L. Sullivan; Simon Pierce (second edition)
Editor: Jennifer Lombardo
Copyeditor: Danielle Haynes
Designer: Andrea Davison-Bartolotta

The photographs in this book are used by permission and through the courtesy of: Cover CraigRJD/istockphoto.com; p. 4 CJ Nattanai/Shutterstock.com; p. 5 raker/Shutterstock.com; p. 6 Rainer Lesniewski/Shutterstock.com; p. 7 Stock for you/Shutterstock.com; p. 8 Marco Gallo/Shutterstock.com; p. 9 oliverdelahaye/Shutterstock.com; p. 10 Sean Pavone/Shutterstock.com; p. 11 Paul Froggatt/Shutterstock.com; p. 12 MISTER DIN/Shutterstock.com; p. 13 Framesira/Shutterstock.com; p. 15 (top) Tigger11th/Shutterstock.com; p. 15 (bottom) wind_dongdong/Shutterstock.com; p. 16 T.Dallas/Shutterstock.com; p. 17 Chaiyapak Mankannan/Shutterstock.com; p. 18 Thomas Quack/Shutterstock.com; p. 19 K-Angle/Shutterstock.com; p. 20 LegoCamera/Shutterstock.com; p. 21 Johnathan21/Shutterstock.com; p. 22 Eiko Tsuchiya/Shutterstock.com; p. 23 DiegoMariottini/Shutterstock.com; p. 24 beeboys/Shutterstock.com; p. 25 SUDONG KIM/Shutterstock.com; p. 26 Wirestock Creators/Shutterstock.com; p. 27 Microgen/Shutterstock.com; p. 28 considine/Shutterstock.com; p. 29 gowithstock/Shutterstock.com.

Some of the images in this book illustrate individuals who are models. The depictions do not imply actual situations or events.

CPSIA compliance information: Batch #CW24CSQ: For further information contact Cavendish Square Publishing LLC at 1-877-980-4450.

Printed in the United States of America

Find us on

CONTENTS

INTRODUCTION

South Korea is a peaceful country with a strong **economy**. It's about the same size as the U.S. state of Indiana. However, it has more than seven times as many people! South Korea used to be connected to its neighbor, North Korea. As one country, it was just called Korea. Today, life in the two countries is very different. While South Korea is very free, the North Korean government is very controlling of its people and economy.

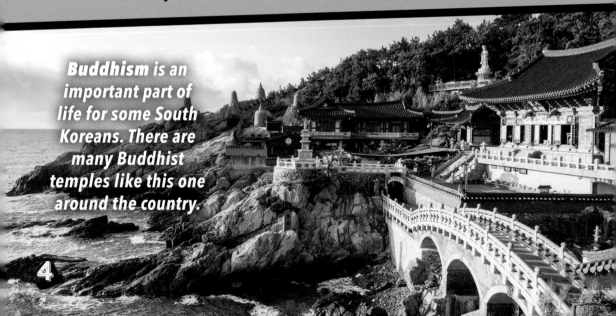

Buddhism is an important part of life for some South Koreans. There are many Buddhist temples like this one around the country.

Over the years, South Korea has combined its own **culture** with Western culture to create something new. For example, visitors can find pizza topped with a Korean food called kimchi.

South Korea is a beautiful place. In the countryside, there are rolling hills dotted with cherry trees. In busy cities such as Seoul, there are many things to do, see, and eat. South Korea is a country with a rich history and a bright future.

South Korea's capital city, Seoul, is in the mountains.

5

GEOGRAPHY

North and South Korea together make up the Korean **Peninsula**. The peninsula is divided at the border of the two countries. To South Korea's east is the Sea of Japan. To its south is the Korea **Strait**. To its west is the Yellow Sea. There are about 3,400 small islands offshore.

This map shows South Korea and its borders.

FACT!
South Korea's largest island is called Jeju Island.

CHINA

Siping
Huadian
Tumen
Vladivostok
RUSSIA

Musan

Shenyang
Tonghua
Chongjin

Ji'an
Kanggye
Kimchaek

NORTH KOREA

Dandong
Sinuiju
Yongbyon
Hamhung

Sohan
Bay
Sunchon
Hungnam
Tonhan
Bay

Korea
Bay
PYONGYANG
Wonsan
Sea of
Japan

Nampo
Songnim

Sariwon
Pyonggang

Changyon

Haeju
Kaesong

Goyang
Chuncheon
Gangneung
Ulleung I.

Bucheon
SEOUL
Seongnam
Incheon
Anyang
Wonju
Ansan
Suwon
Yongin
SOUTH

Pyeongtaek

Cheonan

Cheongju
Gumi

Yellow
Sea
KOREA

Gunsan
Iksan
Pohang

Jeonju
Daegu

Ulsan

Masan
Changwon

Gwangju
Jinju
Gimhae
Busan

Suncheon

Mokpo
Yeosu
Strait

Tsushima I.

Korea

Kitakyushu

Fukuoka

Jeju
Jeju I.
Sasebo
JAPAN

South Korea's mountains are very old.
They're small and covered with trees.

South Korea's major rivers include the Naktong, the Han, and the Geum. There are very few natural lakes, but many man-made ones.

Winters are cold and long, without much snow. Summers are short and hot, with a lot of rain. Sometimes it rains so much that parts of the country flood.

YELLOW DUST

Every spring, winds blow sand from China's deserts into South Korea. This is called "yellow dust" because it often makes the sky look yellow. This time of year makes the air in South Korea very dangerous, or unsafe, to breathe.

HISTORY

People have lived on the Korean Peninsula for about 700,000 years. For some of its early history, the area was divided into three kingdoms that often fought each other. In the late 7th century CE, China helped the Silla kingdom take over the whole peninsula to become one country.

This wall in Gimhae, South Korea, dates back to the Three Kingdoms period. It's part of the remains of an old fort, or military stronghold.

From 1910 until 1945, Japan controlled Korea. After World War II ended in 1945, Korea split into two countries. In 1950, North Korea **invaded** South Korea with the **goal** of taking it over. China helped North Korea, and the United States helped South Korea. The Korean War ended in a stalemate, or tie, in 1953.

This picture shows the DMZ, looking into North Korea. Leaders from the two Koreas meet in the blue houses in the middle. No one is ever allowed to cross the border.

GIVING EACH OTHER SPACE

Between North and South Korea is a 2.4-mile-wide (3.9 kilometer) space called the Demilitarized Zone (DMZ). "Demilitarized" means no military from either country is allowed there. Korean and other world leaders created the DMZ after the Korean War ended.

GOVERNMENT

South Korea's official name is the Republic of Korea. A republic is a kind of government in which the citizens elect people to make their laws. Like the United States, South Korea has three branches of government. The legislative branch makes the laws. In Korea, this is called the National Assembly. The executive branch, which includes the president and prime minister, makes sure people follow the laws. The judicial branch, which includes the courts, decides how the laws apply to real cases.

The National Assembly meets at this building in Seoul.

The president of South Korea can serve only one five-year term. They choose a prime minister. The National Assembly has to authorize the choice.

Voters elected Yoon Suk Yeol as president of South Korea in 2022.

TWO KOREAS, ONE COUNTRY?

North Korea's official name is the Democratic People's Republic of Korea. It's very close to South Korea's official name. Both countries say they are the true Korean government and that the whole peninsula belongs to them.

FACT!
The South Korean prime minister's job is much like the U.S. vice president's job.

11

THE ECONOMY

After the Korean War, South Korea was one of the world's poorest countries. However, the country quickly bounced back. Today, South Korea's economy is the 12th-largest in the world and the 4th-largest in Asia. South Korea sells many things to other countries.

FACT!

Many tourists, or visitors, come to South Korea each year. Tourism fell when COVID-19 spread around the world, but it's rising again as of 2023.

Korean products are shipped all over the world.

Electronics and cars are two important things South Korea makes. Hyundai and Kia cars are from South Korea. Samsung is a Korean company that makes phones, computers, TVs, and other electronics. The country imports, or buys, gas and oil from other countries. Its main trading partners are China, the United States, Japan, and Vietnam.

Shown here are Samsung phones.

SAMSUNG'S SUBSIDIARIES

A subsidiary is a company controlled by a larger company. Samsung has many subsidiaries in South Korea. They include hospitals, theme parks, hotels, and clothing companies. Korea's whole economy would suffer if Samsung failed.

THE ENVIRONMENT

South Korea is home to more than 18,000 species, or kinds, of animals. These include white-naped cranes, lynxes, and minke whales. The Amur leopard and the Asiatic black bear are two Korean animals that are **endangered** because of human activity. Koreans are working to save these two species.

Like the rest of the world, South Korea is facing problems from **climate change**. To try to fix this, the country is working to lower **pollution**. They are using more energy, or power, from the sun and wind so they can use less oil and gas.

FACT!

There used to be many tigers in Korea, but today they're almost all gone. Some may live in the DMZ, but no one knows for sure.

HUMANS, KEEP OUT!

Because people aren't allowed in the DMZ, it's become a safe place for all kinds of animals. More than 5,000 kinds of plants and animals live there, and 106 of those are endangered.

The Asiatic black bear is sometimes called the "moon bear" because of the moon-shaped spot of lighter fur on its chest.

The king cherry tree is a rare, or hard-to-find, kind of cherry tree that grows on Jeju Island.

THE PEOPLE TODAY

Most of South Korea's more than 51 million people live in big cities on the coast. Because there are so many people living in such a small area, the country is very crowded.

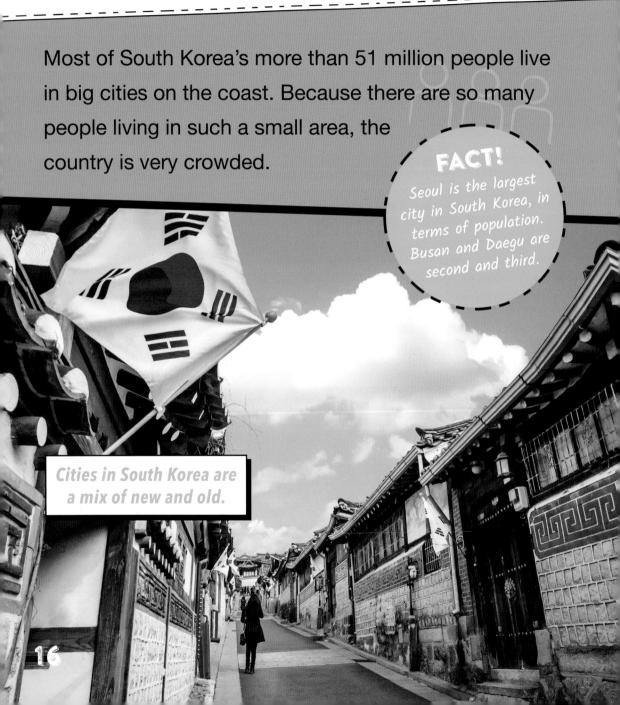

Cities in South Korea are a mix of new and old.

Almost everyone who lives in South Korea is Korean. However, there are small communities of Japanese, Chinese, and Americans.

South Koreans tend to see themselves as one group working toward common goals. Their culture is rooted deeply in the teachings of Confucius, a thinker who created rules for life around 500 BCE. Confucianism says people should honor their family, rulers, and older people. Confucianism isn't a religion, or faith. However, some people treat it that way.

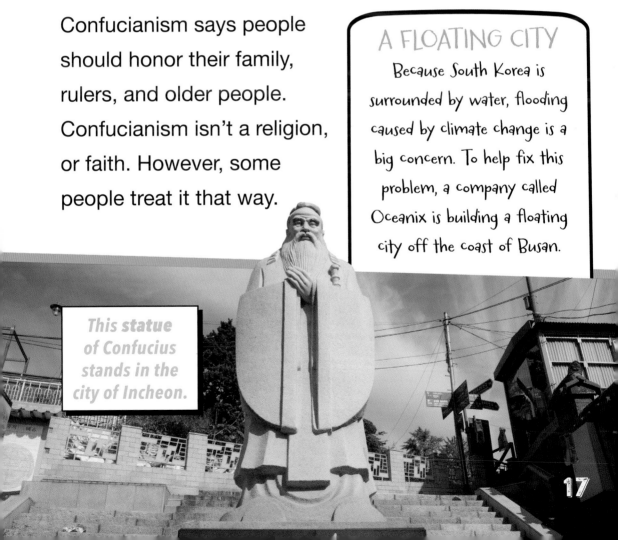

A FLOATING CITY

Because South Korea is surrounded by water, flooding caused by climate change is a big concern. To help fix this problem, a company called Oceanix is building a floating city off the coast of Busan.

This statue of Confucius stands in the city of Incheon.

LIFESTYLE

South Koreans care a lot about **tradition**. They take care to mark certain days with special actions called rites. For example, many Koreans believe that a person's spirit doesn't leave Earth until many years after they've died. For this reason, people perform rites to honor dead parents and grandparents on holidays and on their death day every year.

Hanbok is the traditional Korean clothing for men and women. Most South Koreans today save it for special days, such as weddings.

South Koreans have combined tradition with modern ways of living. Today, women are legally equal to men. Men and women get the same education. However, the country still has problems with sexism. For example, women are paid about 31 percent less than men for the same job.

WELL-EDUCATED

Education is very important in South Korea. Adults push children to get good grades from a very young age. Many South Koreans attend college after high school.

FACT!

A person's 61st birthday and a baby's 100th day of life are special days in South Korea.

South Korean women are often treated poorly if they don't wear makeup or have long hair.

RELIGION

About 56 percent of people in South Korea don't follow any religion. However, everyone in the country is free to follow any religion they want. Most religious people follow Buddhism or Christianity. There are also a few people who follow Islam or shamanism, which is Korea's traditional religion.

FACT!
Most Korean shamans, or traditional spiritual leaders, are women.

Colorful lanterns, or lamps, hang over a Buddhist temple in Seoul.

Korean shamanism was the religion everyone followed before Buddhism and Christianity arrived on the peninsula. Korean shamanists believe there are many gods watching over them. In the past, they would perform special actions to make the gods happy enough to bless the people. Today, people still often ask shamans for help when they need to make an important choice or think they are being haunted by ghosts.

Koreans tied ribbons to this tree to honor the god that watches over their village.

SPREADING CHRISTIANITY

Christianity first came to Korea when Koreans visited China in the 1600s and brought back ideas they learned there. Until the 1900s, Christianity was illegal in Korea. Christians had to meet in secret to practice their faith.

LANGUAGE

Around the world, more than 80 million people speak the Korean language. It is not closely related to any other modern language.

The way Korean is spoken depends on the rank of the speakers. The language uses honorifics. This means there are special words people use when speaking to someone of a different rank. For example, children may use honorifics when speaking to their parents and teachers.

People say Hangul is so easy to learn that it can be mastered in a day. However, being able to read Korean doesn't mean a person can speak the language.

In 1443, an alphabet called Hangul was invented. In 1446, it became Korea's official alphabet. Before that, people wrote Korean with the Chinese alphabet. People of high rank continued to use Chinese until 1945. This is because China still had a lot of **influence** on Korean culture.

EASY TO LEARN

Hangul was meant to be easy to learn quickly. The idea was that everyone should be able to read. The shapes of the alphabet mimic, or copy, the movements a person's mouth makes when saying them.

FACT!

A child can call their parents abeoji and eomeoni (father and mother) or appa and eomma (mom and dad).

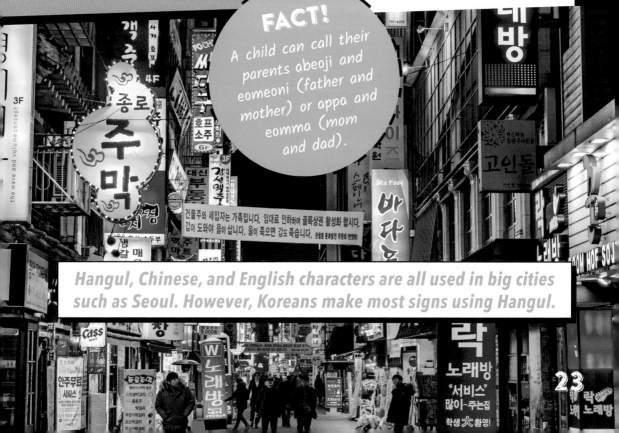

Hangul, Chinese, and English characters are all used in big cities such as Seoul. However, Koreans make most signs using Hangul.

ARTS AND FESTIVALS

South Korea has many kinds of traditional music and dance. Sometimes music, dance, acting, and martial, or fighting, arts are mixed in traditional mask dramas. South Korean traditional painting uses ink on paper and often shows scenes from nature.

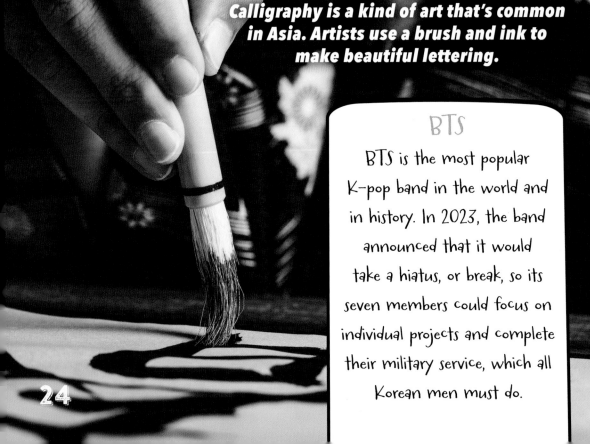

Calligraphy is a kind of art that's common in Asia. Artists use a brush and ink to make beautiful lettering.

BTS

BTS is the most popular K-pop band in the world and in history. In 2023, the band announced that it would take a hiatus, or break, so its seven members could focus on individual projects and complete their military service, which all Korean men must do.

However, as with other parts of its culture, South Korea combines old and new in the arts. Korean pop music (K-pop) is popular all around the world. South Korean TV shows called K-dramas are also very popular in other countries.

Festivals are important times for South Koreans. They include Korean New Year, the first full moon festival, and the harvest festival. People honor the dead on these days and have parties for the living.

Since 1998, people have traveled to the city of Boryeong for its yearly Mud Festival.

FUN AND PLAY

South Koreans enjoy many of the same activities as people in other countries. Watching and playing sports, going to the movies, and playing video games are all very popular there. Many people also enjoy playing traditional South Korean musical instruments.

FACT!

Seoul was home to the 1988 Summer Olympics, and PyeongChang hosted the 2018 Winter Olympics.

Many Korean families enjoy spending the day at a theme park.

Families love to spend time in nature. They enjoy walking, hiking, or fishing. There are even good places to ski and snowboard.

South Korea has several kinds of martial arts that are popular around the world. Tae kwon do is one of the most famous. It became an Olympic sport in 2000. Hapkido and Taekkyeon are two other martial arts styles.

GAMES AS SPORTS

Video game matches, or e-sports, have grown in popularity around the world since the beginning of the 2000s. Choices made by the South Korean government at that time helped make the country the center of the e-sports world.

Tae kwon do is a popular sport for kids as well as adults.

FOOD

Although Western dishes can be found in South Korea, many Koreans prefer their traditional foods. Most of the popular dishes are based on grains and vegetables. Rice, beans, and hot peppers are very popular. Since there is such a long coastline, seafood is also common.

FACT!

The egg in bibimbap is often served raw. However, some people fry it first.

Shown here are some common Korean dishes. Many Koreans like their food spicy.

Bibimbap and kimchi are two popular dishes that can be found all over the country. Bibimbap is a bowl of rice topped with vegetables, beef or chicken, and an egg. Kimchi is made of **fermented** vegetables, especially cabbage. It can be eaten on its own or used as a topping. Some of the most popular desserts are made from rice and sweetened bean paste.

A SPECIAL KOREAN DISH

People have been eating kimchi for more than 2,000 years. It's a food many people think of when they picture Korean food. When Koreans smile for pictures, they don't say "cheese," they say "kimchi"!

Kimchi pancakes are a popular food, and they aren't just for breakfast.

GLOSSARY

Buddhism: A religion of eastern and central Asia that came from the teaching of Siddhartha Gautama (Buddha).

climate change: A change in the Earth's weather patterns over time, which can be caused by human activity.

culture: The beliefs and ways of life of a group of people.

economy: The way goods and services are made and sold.

endangered: At risk of dying out.

fermented: Describing something that is acted on by bacteria or yeast to produce a sour, preserved kind of food or drink.

goal: The object toward which effort is directed.

influence: An effect one thing has on another.

invade: To enter a place by force, often with the goal of taking it over.

peninsula: A piece of land that is surrounded by water on three sides.

pollution: Man-made waste that makes the air, ground, or water dirty or unsafe.

statue: A likeness sculptured, modeled, or cast in a solid surface.

strait: A narrow channel connecting two bodies of water.

tradition: A way of thinking, behaving, or doing something that's been used by people in a society for a long time.

FIND OUT MORE

Books

Dickmann, Nancy. *Your Passport to South Korea.* North Mankato, MN: Capstone Press, 2021.

Klepeis, Alicia. *South Korea.* Minneapolis, MN: Bellwether Media, 2020.

Wood, John. *A Visit to South Korea.* Minneapolis, MN: Bearport Publishing, 2023.

Websites

Kids World Travel Guide: South Korea
www.kids-world-travel-guide.com/south-korea-facts.html
Read more about South Korea, and take a look at some beautiful pictures.

National Geographic Kids: South Korea
kids.nationalgeographic.com/geography/countries/article/south-korea
Learn more cool facts about South Korea.

Video

YouTube: "Introducing South Korea"
https://www.youtube.com/watch?v=KBCuJ_2wWPU
Get a quick overview of what it's like to visit South Korea.

Publisher's note to educators and parents: Our editors have carefully reviewed these websites to ensure to ensure that they are suitable for students. Many websites change frequently, however, and we cannot guarantee that a site's future contents will continue to meet our high standards of quality and educational value. Be advised that students should be closely supervised whenever they access the internet.

INDEX

32